POEMS
1947-1961

By

Eʟɪᴢᴀʙᴇᴛʜ Sᴇᴡᴇʟʟ

Chapel Hill

THE UNIVERSITY OF NORTH CAROLINA PRESS

CONTEMPORARY POETRY SERIES

Manufactured in the United States of America

Poems in this collection have appeared in *The Aylesford Review, The Cambridge Review,* and *The Tablet* in England, *The Pylon* in Rome, and *Thought* and *Commonweal* in the United States. The poet's grateful thanks are due to the editors of these journals for permission to reprint; to Chatto and Windus, London, for permission to reprint "Babylon" from *The Field of Nonsense;* and to the Director of Yale University Press for permission to include the group of thirteen poems that form Part V of *The Orphic Voice.*

PRINTED BY THE SEEMAN PRINTERY, DURHAM, N. C.

CONTENTS

POEMS
1947-1961

JOB

They did not know this face
Where the chin rested on the sunken breastbone,
  So changed it was, emptied, rinsed out and dried,
  And for some future purpose put aside.
Expecting torment, they were much perplexed.

His world had gone
And he sat isolated, foul and flyblown,
  Without a world, with nothing but a mind
  Staggered to silence since it could not find
Language to utter its amazing text.

For where was Job?
In some strange state, unknown and yet well-known,
  A mask that stared hollowly in God's breath,
  Mind that perceived the irrelevance of death,
And the astonished heart unmoved, unvexed.

They did not see his soul
Perched like a bird upon the broken hearthstone,
  Piping incessantly above the ashes
What next what next what next what next what next

ARCHANGELS IN WINTER

They are not as the snow,
Soft, fluted, curled.
They are not as the sky,
Glacier-blue.
Yet in a figured show
One knows them too,
Watching the hawks that fly
Above the world.

Their wings are not as these,
Brown, feathered, taut;
No need to crouch beside
The cowering hare.
Yet human flesh is caught
And terrified,
And hare and human freeze,
Watching them there.

They follow other laws.
Held in a drift,
No snowbound mind can hope
To visualize
This sense of preying claws
And hooded eyes,
Where iris shadows shift
Across the slope.

Their being will not fuse
With Arctic storms
Or Borealis flare
Of whites and blues:
But keen minds light the air
With intellectual forms—
Perhaps Pythagoras' square
On the hypotenuse.

CHARM FOR A LOGICIAN

Five fruitless years the man had spent
With *Darii* and *Celarent*;
His *Ferio* was out of joint,
Bocardo, too had lost its point,
Felapton, his familiar, dumb,
And all the world a vacuum,
The mind relating stress to stress
In aching webs of emptiness,
And he must find some exorcism
For the obsessive syllogism.

Now by some fit of madness drawn,
He has gone out across the lawn,
And there beneath the orchard trees,
Between two candles, on his knees,
Saw the green glooms of summer weather
Grow tiny crests of candle feather,
And fingertip mock-orange fruit
Bubble upon each loaded shoot
Of silver twigs for candle flames,
And birds appeared with unknown names,
Soft grey-blue, with the rounded shapes
Of shot-silk green and purple grapes;
Thirst slaked with mulberries and limes,
His throat was murmuring nursery rhymes,
Repeated in the crooning call
Of peachbloom pigeons on the wall,
And through the figs and jargonnels
Flamed kingfishers and cardinals,
And candle light and greenleaf mesh
Came back again in melon flesh,
The olive and flamingo hoops
Of honeydews and cantelupes,
And creatures of pomegranate stuff,
Grey woodpeckers with cherry ruff,
Whose beak, a black stiletto, picks
The smooth-stemmed silver candlesticks.

A lunatic logician sees
No nets for birds, no nets for trees,
And cries among the loosened knots—
A Phoenix in the apricots.

BABYLON

They built their fortunes with a pack of cards,
A tower of cards, breathless scaffolding of chance;
They built their tower to make the stars dance
A tiptoe on its parapet;
Heel and toe they were to go
In Babylon along the crenellations
To old priests' incantations.
Very haughty these were, but at their prayer
The stars might leave their shoes on the topmost stair—
But the stars burst their shoestrings and all their feet were bare,
Dancing to the tune the old cards were calling,
(King and Emperor and Pope),
Handled hieratically, a horoscope,
Centuried games of patience, the zodiac falling
Into constellated suits of red and black
Until God smote them with the coming of day,
Lime-green and heliotrope,
And all the pack went whirling
Into a wounded sky,
Sandstorm of emblems, sky-cloud lightened and thundered,
And God sundered them in the cold of the morning air
And the majesty of their mouths moving.

The stars put on their shoes,
Soberly disposed.
Cock crows
Dimpling across the stoneyards
Where dirty folk yawn and stretch their elbows.
But we hold back the dawn
Hours upon hours,
Threescore years or threescore miles and ten,
By starlight dancing our way to broken towers
With little candles our swirling twirling skirts have blown about,
And in our dance of words the stars pop in and out,
And God smiles sleepily and you see Him reach
His Hand—for what? But already the stars have lost their track
And farandole to our rigmarole,
For in my pocket I have that ancient pack,
(King and Emperor and Pope),
And dance for ever on Babylon's plain,
In tight star-figures, shuffling the cards of speech
In a mountebank brain,
Fearing demoniac powers
But in celestial hope
To wind God back into the dance again.

OPEN AIR CONCERT, OHIO

We sit by stone and ivy leaves
For flute and oboe's disquisition;
The evening, after heat, receives
This gentle Middle West rendition.

The foursquare walls of courtyard cup
Two funnels at their intersection,
The music running down and up
On lukewarm currents of convection,

So that the twin parabola
Of clarinettists' conversation
May tunnel for mandragora
Or plummet to a constellation.

The body may be earthed or skied,
But mind, extrinsic to seduction,
Spreads out into a thin glass slide,
Incising music's cones of suction.

O leave those twinkling points to pair
With ground bass in a Bach Invention:
Cry me not up to meet them there—
I balance on my disc of air—
In a glass darkly I shall stare
At inklings of a fourth dimension.

BALLADE

For a Popular Preacher

Your entry pat upon your cue;
Those handout programme notes which bear
Your converts' names (the well-to-do)
For titbits on the bill of fare;
The casual way you chose to wear
That cloak of Tyrian purple hue,
Manoeuvred with an actor's flair—
Was this the best that you could do?

The microphone you seemed to woo
Like Frank Sinatra in despair;
The jokes, some even against *you*,
In which we were allowed to share;
That gesturing dramatic air,
Blood-curdling thrills or *billet-doux*,
Those flashing eyes, that floating hair—
Was this the best that you could do?

Your audience hadn't got a clue,
Of which no doubt you were aware,
And so you cheapened all you knew,
But even so, to stand up there
So buxom, blithe and debonair
And give us pinchbeck coin for true,
Assuming nobody would care—
Was this the best that you could do?

ENVOI

Monsignor, idol of the fair,
Of matinées at half-past two,
I grudge that dollar for my chair—
Was this the best that you could do?

TWO SONGS FOR SAINTS

I. For Saint Thomas Aquinas

The Owl and the Pussy-cat went to sea
    With the Duck and the Kangaroo
And the Quangle-Quee and the Crumpetty Tree
    And Saint Thomas Aquinas too.
On the shining wharf they loaded him in
    As they rocked on Heaven's moat,
And the ballast he offered them made them laugh,
The *Summa*, in folio, bound in calf,
Saint Thomas being too big by half
    For the beautiful pea-green boat.

They played, to please his saintly ear,
    Their little coppery gong,
As they sailed away for a year and a day,
    And nobody found it long,
For skirting around the Chankly Bore
    Or the Lands where the Jumblies live,
There was always something to see and hear
When Rimbaud's *bateau ivre* drew near,
Or they spied the Ancient Marineer
    Sailing by in a sieve.

They've given him muffins and lollipop rice
    Under the light of the moon;
He's given them milk of Paradise
    Out of a runcible spoon;
For logic and nonsense share their love,
    To give or to receive,
And the tiny Pobble who has no toes,
And the sorrowful Dong with the Luminous Nose
Have a warm and comforting place to doze
    In a saint's enormous sleeve.

O who comes gliding up the sky
    To drowse the northern star
With *Lauda Sion* for lullaby
    To the strains of a small guitar?
Is it the Ark, or Peter's Barque
    With all sail set for Rome?
No, not a vessel as grand as that—
It's nothing at all to be wondered at—
It's only the Owl and the Pussy-cat
    Sailing Saint Thomas home.

London Bridge is broken down,
(Dance over, my lady lee),
And little wonder
Beneath the thunder
Of all this glorious company,
Some in rags
And some in tags
And some in silken gown.
The stately ships came sailing in,
The birds began to sing,
And all the Saints came dancing, dancing,
(Come up to London to see the Queen!)
This cold and frosty weather;
The bells shall ring,
The steeples swing,
And we clap hands together.
Silver bells
And cockle shells
For Saint James of Compostella,
Saint Francis Xavier with his umbrella,
Out of England I saw them dance,
Out of England into France,
Out of France into Spain
Then back to Gloster
For a Paternoster
All in a shower of rain,
To Banbury Cross
And Walsingham,
And so to London once again.
One foot up and one foot down,
See how they dance in London Town!

The fiddles squeak, the bagpipes snore,
Seven swans a-swimming along Chelsea shore
Where Saint Thomas More
May dance at his ease
In and out the golden pear and silver apple trees.
(Applethorn and appleseed,
God send us comfort in our need!)
Green gravel,
Green gravel,
The grass is so green,
And the dancing here goes bright as day
To the lilt of Saint Teresa's tambourine:
Come out to play,
Come out to play,
Come to the baker's to buy you some bread;

But abed
Lies many a sleepyhead,
Stick stock stone dead,
Safe between sheets upstairs
The gooseygander old men who will not say their prayers,
And Anthony Rowley says Heigh-ho
While the Saints go dancing in their blood and fire,
With sweetbriar
And bonfire
And strawberry wire,
In a ring o' roses round they go.

Saint Francis
Dances
With the neat Saint Giles
All about the rooftops (brickbats and tiles)
Up above the crooked men who go their crooked miles.
Here come Saint Clement's
Oranges and lemons!
Here come Saint Anne's
Kettles and pans,
Making a joyful din,
(God save all pride and sin!)
Turn about and turn about and bring a new year in!
A, B, C,
Tumbledown D,
Upon Paul's steeple stands a Tree
Where sits the Queen (she sits in the sun),
Seventeen, eighteen,
Maids-in-waiting,
Mary, with the Blessed Lamb Whose fleece is white as snow,
And round and round the burning bush the heavenly dancers go.
Gay go up and gay go down,
Up to Heaven from London Town.
The heart must break, the sky will fall—
To this dear dance God bring us all—
Come back, Peter!
Come back, Paul!

THE GREAT DARKNESS

A Play for Voices

Characters: Abraham
Isaac, his son
Kemuel, his servant

(*A woman's voice*)

You know as well as I
Darkness is not just the sun gone out of the sky.
You know, too, though you may not choose to remember,
Darkness as something intimate and near,
Not the long nights advancing to December
And then retreating slowly half a year.
You too have understood: darkness can lie
Behind the observer's eye,
A great darkness indeed.

I am not asking you to rehearse again
That darkness you have known,
Some passionate bewilderment or pain,
The aching in the bone,
Which you have suffered and, you thought, alone.
It's only this I tell—
That there's no edge to the darkness of the mind;
We're all in it as well,
And these three,
Abraham, Isaac, Kemuel
(That's what I've called the servant).
It's only a play
And that's as it should be,
But something lies behind
That story in Genesis; that's why I say
"Shut your eyes and listen. No-one can hope to see
Through midnight wilderness of heart and mind.
Admit as much: one might as well be blind,
Confused in that great darkness, even as they."
But if you'll venture there,
By ear, by words, into this desert place,
"A horror of great darkness"—so the phrase runs
In the Bible—somebody might find
An answer somewhere and lift up a face,
Someone in the play perhaps, Abraham or his son,
Or you or I.
I'd ask your prayers
If you'd not think it strange, and pray for you,
Most simply, for God's grace

Upon us all,
For now His own clear clouds of darkness fall
On mind and heart
And over the plains of Mamre and Esdraelon, the land of Moriah,
Canaan, Philistia, Salem and the salt sea.
All things are gone, gone under with the sun.
There's only darkness—and a play begun.

ISAAC   (*A young voice but not a child's*)

> Kemuel! Don't fall over the sticks!
> I've put them down here. That's right, catch hold of
> my hand.
> Kemuel! This *is* you, isn't it?

KEMUEL   (*A strong man's voice*)

> Yes, of course it is.
> Who else could it be in all this desert land?
> Your father's over there,
> Waited behind where the hill falls away,
> Said he must say a prayer.
> (*Soothingly*) He'll be here soon.
> Look up, Isaac! It's not as dark as you might think.
> Even if there is no moon
> There are a few stars anyway,
> And Abraham watching them, as he's always done.

ISAAC   Kemuel . . . do you think we could make a fire?

KEMUEL   It's for you to say, not me after all, son.
> Only I had the feeling your father wanted the wood
> For something else, something special—
> The wood you've been carrying all day.
> But if you say so, well and good.

ISAAC   I've lost the bundle for the moment.
> Where's it gone?
> No, don't leave go of my hand, we'll look for it two
> and two.
> It's very queer that it's so dark.
> If we weren't holding hands I'd lose you too
> And have to grope for you as well as the sticks.
> Don't pull in the wrong direction, Kemuel!
> (*Laughing, but nervously*) How silly this is—and you're
> like a stubborn horse!
> *This* way!
> (*A loud rattle*) Ow!

KEMUEL	What's happened?
ISAAC	The sticks! I've found them! Kemuel, my shin! It'll never be the same again! Well, here they are anyhow. Yes, that's right, long and thin . . . I've got the bundle with both hands now, Quantities of faggots. There must be just this pattern down my back. Long furrows. What did you do with your pack, Kemuel?
KEMUEL	Kept it on—I've got more sense than you. No good setting things down in this dark night.
ISAAC	You're right, of course. Let's slip a faggot or two Out of the bundle. Father can't miss those And we could make a *little* fire, only a little one, So I could see my feet, Kemuel,—so I could just see my nose!
KEMUEL	Funny thing to do! (*Changing his tone*) Don't shake so, Isaac. You, old Abraham's son, And afraid of the dark? Why, he knows all about the night, The way the stars move . . . he's almost friends with them. (*Snaps a stick or two*) What a noise these sticks make! Still, they're good and dry. He talks to God, like this, through the night sky; They say God answers him; but you and I, We wouldn't know, would we? Look, my dear, Here comes a little flame and another here! Aren't I good at fire-making, Isaac? Sit down beside it, youngster, and stop shaking.
ISAAC	(*His teeth chattering*) Sorry, Kemuel. I don't think it's really fear, Only I'm tired and I don't know why we're here And so I'm puzzled too. Still, it's lovely to be able to see you again. Not that I can see much, but never mind, It's better than being absolutely blind. The darkness is pushed back a little bit And gives one room for breathing.
KEMUEL	Do you see your father?
ISAAC	No. Where?
KEMUEL	That way. He's standing over there,

The light just catching his white beard and hair
And the pattern in the long robe,
Kind of peacock's eyes in the weaving.
Your mother made it.
She takes a pride in that. The other,
Now she couldn't do a thing that way;
Dancing or singing, yes, or looking at you out of the long
    black lashes
Of her Egyptian eyes, wide and unblinking, till you often
    wondered
What she was thinking. But no-one knew.

ISAAC   Who are you talking about, Kemuel? Is it really true
What some of them say in the camp, that there was
    someone else,
Someone who was Father's wife before I was born?

KEMUEL   There were . . . the two.

ISAAC   Both of them at once? I can't quite understand.

KEMUEL   *(half to himself)* I didn't either. *Two* of them in hand!
One woman's quite enough.
I shouldn't perhaps have mentioned it; and then they're
    dead.

ISAAC   They, Kemuel? Who are *they*?

KEMUEL   I don't want to talk about it, Isaac.
What made me begin?
Maybe just the sight of the old man
Standing out there against the night;
Only I've seen him so often looking just like that on
    coming in
Out of the darkness and the desert sand,
From going the round of the flocks and herds,
Having an eye to us, servants like children to him,
Born in his service. He had friendly words
For each of us, knew every one by name;
He'd ask after your woman and when the baby came.
Out of the dark he'd come.

*(A silence. In the distance Abraham's voice is heard, very deep and firm
but sounding a long way off.)*

ABRAHAM Not head or heart, God: only hands can pray
In such extremity, as between friends
Where touch is language, and each comprehends
What the mute body's gestures would convey,

The supplication of the finger-ends,
Suffering skin-tips to the Milky Way.
What milk of human tears runs from the stars
To stanch the heart love's fires consume away?

ISAAC Kemuel, did you hear?

KEMUEL Not all, and understood not all of that.
He's praying, Isaac. Something's on his mind.
Love, he said. What's love to God, I wonder?
I could think of God as a good master,
An old wise king
Like Abraham himself among his flocks,
Or something terrible, wind, lightning and thunder
Smiting the rocks.
But love—that's another thing.

ISAAC But Father loves us all!
I don't see why it's so different. Tell me why.

KEMUEL I wasn't thinking of that kind of love.
That isn't to deny
The old man's kindness—but I meant something else.

ISAAC What?

KEMUEL Between men and women then, if you must know.
But you're too young.

ISAAC I'm not a child, Kemuel, truly not.
I know—well, that men and women come together
And children are born from them.
You have a little son yourself, Kemuel, haven't you?
What is it like to be married?

KEMUEL I find it hard to say.
Like all other marriages, I suppose.
You remember your wedding day
And your wedding night, and then after that
It settles down into a steady warmth;
It's like good food, a roof against the weather,
Or like a fire, welcoming and cheering
At the day's close.

ISAAC Our fire's nearly out. Shall we let it go?
Better not use any more sticks
If Father wants them. I'll stir it up. Look, there's a
  little glow;

It'll last another half-hour maybe,
Keep us a little longer from the night.

KEMUEL   I can see your father again now,
Still standing there in this uncertain light
That will so soon be dead.

ABRAHAM   (*from a distance, as before*)

Fires underneath the stars, disparity,
The cold impassive and the hot and blind;
For diamond eyes and frozen clarity
Of reason in divine or human mind
Blessed be God—but heart, where shall we find
Some homelier flame lambent with charity
To fuse this midnight chaos into one,
God and a death, fires starcrost and undone,
Dismay in darkness for an only son.

ISAAC   Did you hear what he said?

KEMUEL   Yes, I did. I think his mind is running back
Like mine, to earlier times, to Ishmael;
He had a son, you see, before you, Isaac,
And loved him dearly,
Then lost him.

ISAAC   Oh. By the other woman. What was she called?

KEMUEL   Hagar.

ISAAC   Hagar and Ishmael. But they're dead.
So is the fire, nearly.

KEMUEL   A woman is like a fire.

ISAAC   Don't stare out so into the darkness, Kemuel.
You can't see anything and the light of the fire comes up
    so queerly
On to your face. And anyway
That was a funny thing for you to say.
Why is a fire like a woman? What can you have meant?
Is it . . . because she's always having to be fed?

KEMUEL   (*laughing*) No!
I don't know myself just what was in my head.
Something to do with this scene
Tonight that keeps reminding me of times gone by,
When Abraham first took Hagar to his tent.

ISAAC	Was she his wife then? Kemuel, this must have been A long long time ago!
KEMUEL	Yes, perhaps it was. But tonight It seems like . . . the day before yesterday. Then there was firelight too that came and went On his hands and face As he came in from the dark of the camp; Sara was in her own place, under the lamp, Sitting embroidering, white leaves upon gold, Some festival attire For Abraham her lord. But Hagar waited for him Beside the fire, And that's how I remember her, Bright firelight on her sharply shadowed face, And she in scarlet, shot with warmth and grace, Openly welcoming a man's desire. And for a time Abraham seemed . . . less old.
ISAAC	Look, Kemuel (silly saying look When you can hardly see a single thing) But isn't that Father coming?
KEMUEL	It might be.
ISAAC	There's something moving. Listen! Can't you hear? Kemuel, suppose it isn't Father. Suppose it's . . . some- thing else? It's desperately dark.
KEMUEL	Well, the only other thing it could be, Apart from God and meaning no blasphemy, Would be the donkey. (*Isaac giggles*)
ABRAHAM	(*calling*) Where are you, my children?
ISAAC KEMUEL	} We're here! Here we are!
ABRAHAM	Yes, I can see you now. God bless you both! Isaac my dear! Kemuel! Have you kept my youngster in good heart?
KEMUEL	I hope so, lord Abraham. Only the fire has nearly gone.
ISAAC	Father, how lovely that you've come. We can be happy now.
KEMUEL	I'll go and sleep, if there's no more I can do.

How early in the morning do we start?

ABRAHAM   (*slowly*) I think you will stay
With the donkey, Kemuel. We two will go on,
The lad and I. But you,
Kemuel, you can sleep. Yes, sleep for you.
Goodnight, my child. Is this you I can feel
Here beside me? You are a good friend. Yes surely, kneel
And have my blessing, as indeed you do.

ISAAC   Goodnight, Kemuel.

KEMUEL   And to you too,
Young Isaac.

ISAAC   Goodnight. Sleep well.

(*A short pause*)

Two steps and then he vanished.
Father dear, are you cold?
I wish I had kept the fire up, but we thought
You wanted firewood for tomorrow. Were we right?

ABRAHAM   Yes, you were right, my son.

ISAAC   Only now it's chilly and your bones are old.
You seem to be shaking.

ABRAHAM   It's nothing, nothing. Only a gust of sorrow
Such as one has after a hundred years
Upon God's earth.

ISAAC   A sorrow? Could you tell me?

ABRAHAM   Not tonight.

ISAAC   Look, I'll come and sit very close beside you
And keep you warm and then the sorrow will go,
Like a poultice for a tooth that's aching!

ABRAHAM   Creep underneath my cloak.
Come next my heart. Have you a mind to sleep?

ISAAC   Not yet, Father. This is the cloak with all the peacocks'
   eyes
Worked on it, isn't it? They're looking out
Over my head now, peacocks' eyes and stars
Having a staring match, neither side blinking;

And then of course no tears—they couldn't weep.
Is that how God looks at us? Steady and thinking?

ABRAHAM   I don't believe so.

ISAAC   How would He look?

ABRAHAM   As I look down at you, perhaps, this minute.

ISAAC   But I can't see you.

ABRAHAM   But you know; you know.

ISAAC   (*sighing*) Yes, Father, so I do. We are so warm and close.
Do you feel better now? I was afraid
You might be feeling ill.

ABRAHAM   No, my age troubles me little.

ISAAC   It must be wonderful to be so old.
All those long years for wisdom and God's will
While the stars circle and come round again,
Knowing all about everything, people and things,
Poems and prayers and stories men have told,
Friendly with God, neighbour to priests and kings;
So long to know so much.

ABRAHAM   So long in pain.

ISAAC   Why do you say that? Not while I am here.
I shall look after you. Feel my arm
Here round your back for comfort and protection.

ABRAHAM   (*after a slight pause*) God will look after me . . . after
us both.

ISAAC   I'm sorry, Father dear. I meant no harm.

ABRAHAM   Of course not. Don't move, Isaac. Bring your cheek
Back to the place it had against my heart.
I meant you no reproach.
You'll play your part;
And I, God helping me, I will play mine.

ISAAC   Isn't this wonderful, to sit so comfortably
The two of us, like this? It seems a shame to speak
Almost. Your heart goes bump bump peacefully
As if we were . . . one person and not two.

ABRAHAM	So we are, in a sense. You, my beloved son— You are my flesh and blood, when all's said and done.
ISAAC	And Mother's too.
ABRAHAM	Yes, hers as well. (*A pause*). She—what will she do?
ISAAC	Do you mean what *is* she doing here and now? I was just wondering that. Do you think she's lying Nicely asleep on her bright carpet bed? Father, she wouldn't . . . I hope she isn't crying. She'd miss us, wouldn't she? Or anyway miss *you*, Like Kemuel's wife; she'd mind his being away. He told me about her tonight, before you came.
ABRAHAM	What did he say? He is most blest In his little Tirzah; she has given him one son And soon there will be another.
ISAAC	He tried to tell me what being married was like, But I was stupid and didn't understand. You could tell me better, couldn't you, about my mother?
ABRAHAM	She was beautiful As she is still, a kind of inner light, Like a lamp shining quietly where one should be. Oh God, the lamplight on that trusting face!
ISAAC	Blessed be God! Why do you name His Name?
ABRAHAM	Against the darkness in this place tonight.
ISAAC	There's no light on our faces, is there? Do you know, Kemuel said a strange thing, That a woman was like a fire. What did he mean?
ABRAHAM	Of whom did he say it?
ISAAC	Of somebody called Hagar. He said you had her first Before my mother, and she had a son, and they died.
ABRAHAM	It is as well we sit here in the dark. Only one small grey cinder still burns red. Yes, there were two. God knows if they are dead; Knows too why I should feel a shame

That you should learn of it, perhaps to blame
Some wanton darkening of the heart or head.

ISAAC   Is it a story, Father? That's how it sounds.
Tell me about them. I should like to know,
But I shall close my eyes and hear your heart-beats
Rocking me to and fro.
Did you love her, Father? And long ago?

ABRAHAM   Isaac, there's only one way for me to begin,
And to you I swear,
Fruit of my body, dear to me as life,
I meant no sin.
I loved them both, God knows with how much prayer
For both of them, Sara my wife,
And Hagar, her servant, who was to bear
By Divine Will my longed-for son and heir.

ISAAC   You sound so solemn it almost makes me afraid.
Father, tell me quickly—you love me, don't you?
Please say you wanted me, when I was born.

ABRAHAM   There, there!
Isaac, my heart, how could I hold you so,
And run my fingers through your tumbled hair
And tell you lies?
I love you, child, as only a father can,
You, late promised, late conceived.

ISAAC   Oh yes, the angels; Mother told me about them.
You knew I was to come?

ABRAHAM   I did not know. I believed.

ISAAC   Go on, Father. The two women—that seems queer.

ABRAHAM   Then close your eyes
Against the cold fires riddling the skies,
And imagine a vision.
God bade me sacrifice
Five beasts to Him, and having killed, split them in two.
I did, and all day through
Watched over the carcasses and drove away
The vultures hovering, and all the day
I waited by those one-time-living things
That at God's Will myself had done to death;
All day the smell of blood was in my breath
As if I too had been a bird of prey,
And I watched over bruised and broken bodies.

· 22 ·

Two were she-creatures, as God ordered it.
And then the sun went down.

ISAAC Father, may I hold your hand?

ABRAHAM Lie down, little son, your head upon my lap.
No need to fear. I too lay where I fell,
Succumbing suddenly to blood and sleep,
Beside those broken females,
In a horror of great darkness, cold and deep
Such as we too are folded in tonight.
And then to inner sight—
This part is hard to tell—
Appeared a light and a light,
One a lamp and one a furnace flame,
Beams, and smoke. Then God called my name
And told me all was well.
And I awoke
And lo, it was a dream.

ISAAC But what has it to do with . . . them?

ABRAHAM I will try to explain.
Sara I loved as the light of my eyes,
Mate of my soul,
Companion of my thoughts and of my laughter,
Faithful and loving. And for that reason
She gave me the other woman for a season,
Not reckoning what would come after.

ISAAC But what did?

ABRAHAM Hagar was her maid
And Sara had no child, and having none
Gave me her maid that she might bear a son
To me in my old age.

ISAAC Are sons so great a gift?

ABRAHAM They are from God:
And I received Hagar at Sara's hands
And she conceived.
Then at last Sara saw what awaited her,
And Sara hated her,
Made her life wretched, baited her,
But in the end was born Ishmael, my eldest.
When he was fourteen, then you were born,

Almost a miracle, to Sara and myself. But it was Ishmael's doom,
And Hagar's.

ISAAC Father . . . were they slain?

ABRAHAM No, no, not that. But I was blind with pain,
And still I see those two small figures dwindle
Across the burning plain,
Hagar and Ishmael, not to come again.

ISAAC (*Very sleepily*) What happened in the end?

ABRAHAM God watch on all of us
In desolation underneath the sky.

ISAAC I think I'll go to sleep now, Father.
I'm glad they didn't die.
There goes the fire's last spark.
Only the darkness now . . . and you . . . and I . . .

(*A pause*)

ABRAHAM (*softly*) Isaac? Isaac? Asleep already!
Now everything has gone,
The companionable fire, the beloved voice;
Only my child's head lies
Across my sterile thighs,
And sand and stars, bright specks, glint on and on.

God, do not leave me.

We have so often spoken
In just this way, at night in solitude,
Under such stars, in Ur of the Chaldees,
Powder of Pleiades,
Dusting the sky-floor, glancing galaxies
Which God Himself chose as a token
Of my children's multitude.
I had two sons.
Ishmael is gone, to some mysterious land,
And Isaac dies tomorrow, at my hand.
Lord, I would clasp Your Knees,
Traditional attitude
Of supplication.
To understand, dear God, to understand!

You made me so,
Created in your likeness, shaped and taught
By a God's Intellect, deep and aglow

As is this sky with stars.
O grapevine of the universe abroad in light,
Star-clusters dangling on the boughs of night,
And mortal mouths drink in the wine of thought!
Now the eye darkens, with the inner sight.
Is it for having sought
By mind and heart to know
Love and its meaning I am brought so low?

No word from God.
The small winds stir.
Isaac sleeps softly. Praised be God for that.
I think of her—and her.

Both were God's creation,
Hagar, wild creature, pure and passionate,
And Sara, clear and bright as a constellation.
Lamp, stars and fire—and all to be put out!
Darkened, I sit and see
Ruin brought upon them and on their children
By me, by me, meaningless devastation.

Had I to choose?
Neither? One alone?
But *both* were love, through to the heart and the womb
    and the core of the bone.
I was their union, one man to fuse
Their partial destinies.
They gave me all they had—love and a child.
Now hearts are broken, now are children gone.
Isaac still lives, but God's now, not my own;
The stars move on.

Have you knowledge of love, great God of Heaven?

If not, should I suppress
Memories of Hagar moving like a cloud
In loveliness?
In what strange words
She told her dreams and talked of forests where waters
    dark and deep
Bore silent glimmering birds, hooked beaks but brooding
    wings,
And she would deck herself, ears, fingers, dress,
With all bright stones, and gold and amber rings
Swung to the downy apricot of her cheeks.

Great fears she had, would wake in the night to weep
And shake against my shoulder and confess
Her terrors, childlike, between sleep and sleep.
And that small swarthy son that we were given . . .
I let them go. I was all they had
But Sara was frightened of them, and they were driven
Into the wild,
A desperate mother and a fevered child
Dumped under the bushes, mad with thirst,
Abandoned lest his mother see him die.
Ishmael, where are you? Lost in the desert? But so am I!
Ishmael! Ishmael! Oh God, my first-born son!

ISAAC   (*stirring*) Father! I heard a cry.
I had a nasty dream, I think.

ABRAHAM It's all right, Isaac. It's nothing. I am here.
Wait, I will give you a drink
If we can find the way to your mouth, can we?
There, now go to sleep again.

(*A pause*)

Sleep on, my dear.
I'll lay my fingers crossways on your eyes;
You need not search these enigmatic skies
Nor know the morning near.
So rest your young damp head
Under my hands which hold your eyelids to,
Even as tomorrow they will yearn to do
The moment you are dead.

O Holy One,
Not the child and not I—
It is the women tearing at my heart:
Recurrent anguish and a soundless cry
Lost in the black abysses of the sky.
What is a woman left without her son?

Sara I have to face,
Tell her that God chose Isaac to be slain
For sins or for a glory not his own—
Died horribly, in violence, his father consenting.
What supernatural grace,
That seed of pain once sown,
Can numb a soul to rest, or to assenting?
Useless to weep myself, no tears
Can touch this pain, fierce axis through the chest,

The heart transfixed upon the huddled spears.

Isaac my child, forgive me if I lay
Your body down now on the ground; and you—
Be friendly with it, since it must accept
You still more closely in an hour or two.
I must rise up and pray.
The long winds blow, and all the things that slept
Look forward to the day.

Great Lord, have mercy on us.

Men, we are blinded, do not understand
What is God's mind and so by sin deceive
And betray ourselves, and with us, womankind.
Women are nearer truth, perhaps, but they,
Daughters of Eve, must pay
For love distorted, Eden thick with weed.
Unhurt, man and woman stand
And look upon each other with dismay:
Can love be sin? Is this where love must lead?
And oh inexplicably the children bleed.

God, I believe that we are in Your Hand.

Not for us to know
Your hidden Will.
You are a spirit. We, who are to die,
Wonder, had You a Son, must He too go
To a fearful death and leave His mother so?
Forgive us: we know there can be no reply.
All is so still.
First light begins to show.
The trees spread out their branches on the hill,
Cedars of Lebanon, scenting all the sky.

Father, accept our pain into Your Glory.

Look mercifully on Your world of men.
The first beams cherish the little grey clouds and the birds
That perish, no man seeing. No more words.
Glory be to God. Amen. Amen.

(*A pause*)

Isaac! Isaac! Wake up. The day is here.
We go to sacrifice.

ISAAC   (*A little pause between each phrase*)
Yes, I'm awake.
A lovely morning! What are we to take?
The knife, of course, and the wood; I'll carry that. But
    Father dear,
We have no victim . . . Father, do you hear?
We have no victim. What is to be done?

ABRAHAM   God will provide the sacrifice, my son.

DRUNKEN BOAT

From Rimbaud

As I came down the broad indifferent streams,
My rigging sensed no men at the controls:
They'd gone for targets, stripped to Redskin screams,
Spitted to multicoloured totem poles.

Nothing I cared for all that changing crew,
Carrying Flemish corn or English twill.
When all the men were gone the noise went too,
And the broad streams consented to my will.

In the mad chopping slap of tide on tide,
The other winter, I, absorbed child-brain,
Raced! The unmoored Peninsulas that ride
Endure no such triumphant row again.

Big storms have blessed my salt awakenings.
Cork-light I danced those waves, for ten nights clear,
That mill their prey in men's imaginings,
Glad to be free of bull's eye lantern leer.

Like apple in child's mouth, sharp tenderness,
Green water crept into my pinewood shell,
Washed me of blue winestains and vomit mess,
Dissolving rudder and grappling hook as well.

Since then, in the Sea-Poem I am lapped,
The Sea all star-infused and turned to cream,
Eat up the glaucous blue where, pallid, rapt,
Some drowned man floats down downward in a dream;

Where suddenly through red-hot daylight hours
The blue is dyed, pulsed madness in slow motion;
Strong as strong drink, vaster than lyre of ours,
Love's russet verjuice turns the working ocean.

Skies that explode in lightnings, whirlspouts' tension,
Currents and surfs I know: I know day's sinking,
Holy as flight of doves the Dawn's ascension,
And glimpsed the Real behind man's wishful thinking.

I've seen low sun mottled with monstrous themes,
Like actors in old plays time out of mind,
Casting long petrified and purple gleams
At far wave-slats à la Venetian blind.

I dreamt the night jade green, snow-dazzle-drowned,
Sea-kisses surface eyewards, slow to break,
Ineffable sap running its courses round,
And blue-gold phosphor sings itself awake.

Charging like rabid cows, months long I haunted
Cattle-back swells stampeding on the reef;
But how the luminous feet of the Marys daunted
Snorting sea-muzzles—that was past belief!

Bumped against Floridas that leave you gaping,
Flowered with eyes of panthers human-skinned,
And underwater skies sent rainbows draping
Harness to shoals of creatures turquoise-finned.

I saw huge seething swamps, whose rush-net traps
A whole Leviathan rotting to a sponge,
Calms split in two by deluges' collapse,
The edge where distance takes the final plunge.

Cindery skies, pearled waves, suns silvered, glacier-ice,
Hideous smashings down and down brown coves
Where giant serpents eaten up by lice
Drop midnight-musky from contorted groves.

I wanted children there to watch with me
Blue water dolphins, fish—the fish were singing
As I in foam of flowers put to sea,
Fitfully fanned by a tranced breeze's winging.

Worn out by hemispheres and poles I'd doubled,
The sea that sobbed me gently here and there
Sent up her own vague flowers, glass-yellow-bubbled,
And I stayed kneeling, woman-like at prayer . . .

Peninsula upon whose taffrail swings
Bird-quarrelling, bird droppings, blond-eyed squawkers,
I sailed, and still the drowned through my frail strings
Went off downstairs to sleep—o backward walkers! . . .

I, castaway past curved coast's hair-fringed brow,
Wind-whirled to birdless stratospheric height,
Salvage for never a sloop or Hansa scow
My drunken corpse, literally water-tight;

Hazed in a violet setting, go-as-I-would,
Steaming, through the sky's redfire wall I rammed,
Bearing a treat for poets who've been good,
Sun-lichen, sea-snot, delicately jammed;

I, plank that bobbed, with sparking moonlets splashed,
Black seahorse squadrons flanked my crazy gunwales,
When the Julys with blows of cudgels smashed
Indigo skies pitted with white-hot funnels;

I, all a-quiver, heard at fifty league
Behemoth's mating-roar with Maelstroms thicken,
Threading the long still blue's endless fatigue,
For Europe's age-old parapets I sicken!

I've seen star-archipelagoes, Cyclades
Whose dizzying skies were sea-lanes for the taking:
—D'you sleep exiled in cosmic nights like these,
Millions of birds of gold, giant Awaking?—

But there, I've cried too much! Dawn's desolation,
The sun's a bitterness, the moon appalling:
Love's bile wells up in slack intoxication.
To be stove in! O the sea calling, calling!

A child of sorrows squatting on his haunches,
A chill dark pool, and Europe's twilight sky—
These I desire—the night scents where he launches
A boatlet fragile as May butterfly.

Across the wake of schooners, cotton-bearing,
I'll cut no more, drenched in a drowning swoon,
Nor dare flags' arrogance and torches flaring,
Nor swim beneath hell-glares from hulk pontoon.

ELEGY FOR TWO DEAD POETS

All a long rainy winter
I, tree-soul that I am, have slid
The cold flat-tasting water,
    Dutiful,
Down my dull clapper-tongue of wood.
The soaked bark bubbles like a wooden sponge;
    Clumsily my dark branches lunge
Black glistening arms, long mirrors to the sky,
The grey reflected light for coverlid,
Black divers dripping from a river plunge
    Steam up their breath, elastic skin
Shows mental bones and thews, athletic thin,
    Trimmed to foul weather
    Till God make it good.
    I, a tree,
May not deny my own simplicity;
Even when water-loaded winds undid
The formal severity of my unleaved pyramid
    Yet have believed
    That I am beautiful.

Into the earth and under,
Roots may explore the ground,
Each fibred hair a mandible,
The infiltration of a blunt incision,
    Complex of chemicals unwound
    By palping rootlets' hunger,
As my long fingers split the cloudy air,
Inverted roots among the winds' division.
    Irresistible
The downward pressure, earthward bound,
Of limbs knotted, thighs, knees, intertwined,
Grope for earth's bones under the fleshly mud,
    Straining in subterranean thunder
    Until soil bear
Bubbles, droplets, tight-crushed tulip bud,
    Bursts of delight and wonder,
Pert crocus crops that in cold copses flare
To chaffinch song after the Circumcision.
Rest now in peace, deep roots, earth-saturate, blind,
    But not insensible;
With a great tenderness, I, tree, after my kind,
Cradle these corpses, rocked invisible,
    Locked in the roots of mind.

Two, there are two
        Whom I bewail,
Poets, not long since dead,
        I never knew.
Only their essence shares that womb and bed,
        Dark, earthy, thorns and shale,
        To which I drew
All beings that I loved, having no sense
        To make a difference
Between the passions of the heart and head.
        Now in a branching frail
Only washed bones and boughs, run through
        By freshet of dew
Or rain-voice drenching the grass—o nightingale!

How can I shelter you? The driven downpour
        Riddles the ribs of bark,
Sopping the brimming marsh, kingcups and mallows,
        Nibbles the river fringe, lays bare
The withies fingering the pebbled shallows;
        I who am dark
As the long nights in March before the birds begin
Hold the cold rain puddled in roots' cup and cone,
Salt-cellar hollows in a collarbone,
        Dark pool for stars to float in,
Dark tree embalmed with icy rain and resin,
Cinnamon and gold-dust damp in the incense boat
Sift into the smoke-thickening of budding woods,
        Spring tree, pillar of prayer,
Spare fountain lifting towards God and All Hallows.
        What do you make of death
Whose juices are washed out for a tree's food?
        I suck your substance, o most rare,
To whisper later into leaves and words;
Sighing I say to you, how do you fare?
Do you prosper, great ones, who lie lowly?
Do you consent to diminution, share
His furred contentment with the mole, exude
        A slowly melting, secular dissolution?
        I, tree,
        Can offer nothing.
Had you been birds, my winter destitution
Still would have held pursuer and pursued,
Sheltered spurred sparrowhawk, hidden the wren
        In comforting undergrowth;
For such as you I am no resting-place.
The soul a bird—you who were pagans both
Might so have seen it in an antic mood,

And I might set a bowl of cream and curds
To things like harpies with a human face,
        Fearful and holy;
    Or seek you in still emptier resolution
And offer my twigs for flute reeds to the winds, a breath
So near to nothing—you who once were men—
That I might hear you, windwise, sing again,
Whistling and piping grace-notes, ghost mouths filled with air,
    Saluting spirits in the cold rooms of space.

I, tree, am simple; nurtured up in faith
        I simply stand
With arms out to remember how God died;
Tree-fashion I apprehend God on a tree
        And the promise of living water
Made to a woman in the broken shade
By a well's edge in hot green borderland,
        Samaria's passionate daughter.
I, a tree planted by the waterside,
        Although it be not yet,
Shall fall and rot in the reed-matted sand
With wet bird bodies and cold-flowering seeds,
        But meantime hold loving affinity
        With mouths that speak of death—
"Pray for us sinners now and at the hour of our death,"
And whispering fingers, holy-water-wet,
        That tell their wooden beads.
Et exspecto resurrectionem mortuorum: et vitam venturi saeculi.
From the water of baptism to the coffinwood in the mould
We are beloved, and after death soul goes in simplicity
To God Who is Most Simple. This we are told.
        For us this is no difficulty:
Hard to understand, not hard to hold.

        But you—I cannot find you.
You had no knowledge but of evanescence.
One soul I have to seek in circling gyres,
        Your trailing cloudy essence
Caught on the zodiac's spikes whose alien fires
        Are slaked in dark-blue wells,
        Slow sapphire deliquescence
Ice-glanced like eyes, and all the magic spells,
Singing fish and smooth-rubbed chestnut images
Wine-washed to the crowing of the cock
        While the stars faded,
        Till there behind you
Shone your own ghost, old passion jaded

To mantic opalescence,
Dissolved in cold Atlantic phosphorescence,
Mother-of-pearl lipping pelagic shells.
And you, that other, whose bitter brilliance bore
A suffering image on the mirror's floor,
Split the mind's universe, apple of glass,
 On quartz and crystal lodes of fission,
  Only to find its core
 A small snake's exquisite nutrition,
Neat jewelled teeth of ivory and brass,
 Quintessence of a lifetime's inquisition,
  And bled therefor.

 Are they of your imaginings
Or mine—dream landscape, mourning meads?
Into what lunar gardens are we come,
Moth-drifted, stiff with everlastings,
  Reedy Elysium?
Is this where you would choose to be?
Soft flaps of petals browning at the hems,
 Unfruiting cherry spume,
(The only moisture this dry twilight breeds)
 Tumid magnolia bloom,
And mushrooms, tender as an infant's thumb,
 Nestling in long-horned moss.
I hear your footfalls up deserted ways,
Shifting the moony discs of honesty,
Rustle about in skeins of thistlefloss
 And dry-veined sycamore seeds,
Rattle past scratchy cornflower heads, unvisited
 By a whirring of sudden wings,
Scarlet and black, the tiny fife and drum
Of goldfinch armies on autumnal days
Scented with quince; and the pierced plum
Bleeds globules of bee-syrup and ambergum,
 Sugared with glossy beads.
Our dead are resting in the fruitful land,
But you—you never sleep and never shall;
 You who would give your all
For one hour's drowsing by a sun-warmed wall,
Somnambulist among the Solomon's seal
And bitter flags, emblems of kings and queens,
  I see you stand,
Wide-eyed and craving, while your shadow leans,
  Pitiable as a bruise,
Across the forehead of a drained canal.
 I would have steeped a hand
 In salves cordial and bland
And laid it on your head and closed your eyes

To try if love might exorcise
The weeping sap and the snapped balsam rod,
      Commending thus to God
The homeless wandering of the dead.

    Where are you, that I may record
A blessing on you? Not in your world but mine,
In no dry mist of death, but from clouds over the hill
      Whose bursting showers
Spill blithe on the heads of great and little saints,
    Falls the witness I bear
      To you, my benefactors.
For I was thirsty and ye gave me drink;
I was an hungred and ye gave me bread;
In prison and ye visited me; sick
      And ye were there.
    One of the least of these,
    I speak for your charity.
What blessing on your head? What may I do
      Who am unfinished still,
    Bare tree among the trees?
Is there some loss that cannot be restored
In an instant of light, seraphic flame and blue,
Kingfisher flash by a forgotten ford?

In other days surely we should have known
      Our brotherhood.
In some cold chantry, tiny as a grave—
Candid and parchment-like its masonry,
Starched linenfold, altar of painted wood,
      Laurel and damson,
In a nimbus of candles—here I had answered your plea,
    "Pray for my soul",
    As Malory asks and Colet,
Langland and Chaucer—we had understood
How each might do the other good,
And the limber spirit, once the body perished,
    Rest on a living tree,
    Spire-thrust of silver birch,
Super hanc petram . . . forest timber grown
Pillar and finial and cornerstone
      Of Holy Church,
    Birds perching on each ledge,
Tree-creeper up the groining, every stave
    Pendent with green and crimson,
    A fimbriated vestment's edge,
March tassellings, woodpecker crests that fledge
    The limbs of the larch,
Nuthatch sky-blue in the tympanum of an arch,

Thundercloud martin cherished under the eaves,
Woodlark's timbrel and pipe from spandrels of graven leaves,
And highest the Holy Ghost, bright Dove, broods over His own
From the budding architrave.

*   *   *

But not for you the myriad starlings cry
   Their dancing interlude,
   Quick fan sweep or sickle ellipse,
Voluted scrollwork to the saffron sky,
The murmuration of God's multitude
Till heaven seem a sieve through which trickles and drips
Giggle and twitter and kissing, pattering thick
On the thin drumskin membrane of the ear,
The pendent tinkling of a chandelier.
      Not this but solitude
Where owl's fawn-fluffed breast feathering dips
   Afloat on breeze-fluted water
Had consecrated your beatitude,
   And prayer must make its way
Softly as breathing water licks its lips
     (*Memento etiam, Domine . . .*)
Or the flame whispers at the candlewick,
Lest you should be estranged by gratitude.

   And since I took to praying for you,
The winter softens, and the melted snow
Meets the counter-advances of a fire,
Sap branched and flaring to the clouded glow
Of storm and sun in equinoctial dawn,
     While bough and bud
   Burning with incandescent blood
Stretch fingers into leaves: I grow, I grow!
     If I have wondered
Lest you were prisoned in a pool of flame,
Shut out from God, blaspheming on His Name,
By your own desire; if begged that He allow
One drop on a little finger hung, to cool
A tawny tongue or hiss on a molten brow,
     I am a fool.
This is no sterile fire out of your veins
    That I have drawn,
Uprushing to a bright tip, flickering spire,
Meeting-point of flame and fountain of winter rains
Over robins' throats in choir that ruddy the steaming lanes,
   And water wagtails paddling on the lawn.

The flames of purgatory have lit the spring,
  Three-branching hazel rods to hold
    Candles of catkin and palm,
A trinity of wands, cambered and twining,
For torch processional or water-divining,
Blossoming into sprigs of prunus and almond sprays
    And all the birds to sing
    Among enchanted trees
After *Asperges*, April-soaked and shining;
  Suffuse the air, where branches' gold
And amber burgeons, silk on cherry bark,
Folds of laburnum brocade in pollen-laden air,
Blaze at the font brimming with water and balm,
  Rim of anemones for forest ponds
In odorem suavitatis, the young woods at prayer.
    Tree, I am grown a tree
Lit with new fire-fronds bursting from wet green twigs,
(*Lux aeterna luceat eis, Domine:*
Cum Sanctis tuis in aeternum; quia pius es.)
  Wild Paschal grace in showers,
Wet sparks brushed by a blown bird's wing,
Fountain of purification, fire over the flowers.

Lover and loved are one: so you and I
  Are purged and pruned for fruit;
But by what water, under what broad sky
  May poetry take root?
Into what country have we sung our way,
  To stand
In wonder and dismay:
  What is this land?
Only in likeness and similitude
  Our mouths have spoken;
Now by one instant of infinitude
  The verse is broken,
And from a broken body poured
  Sweet water, living fire,
Too fierce a splendour, shot with hail and sleet—
Gloria in excelsis the tongue babbled,
The words poor kindling on that Phoenix pyre.
  The little birds are nesting,
  The world's green forests resting,
And sun and rain over the universe,
But we must wait a Rising, blood-bedabbled,
  Until we have adored,
Asking that we in the heart have Christ Our Lord
And in the mouth an innocence of verse.

THE ANALOGUE

I ask my words
For livelier ways,
(I am to blame
That let them stiffen)—go
Over the waterfall
And tumble on the smooth bones
Of the rocks, beat, beat,
The damp air carrying all
The smells of summer, hot and blue,
White spiders bracketing green fern,
And the short cries of birds.

Even so,
Heart, think no shame
To lie among the parched stones,
Feeling the glassy pulses of the heat.
How I must call
The kindling body to its silent mime
I do not know,
But I shall learn—
Find every creature's time,
Cricket-chirp minute,
Shake down my hair and let it blow
Among the greening willows,
Or scratch my hard nail down a twig's horny shell
And bleed with the sap in it.

Gently undo
The sinews of our rhythms. Set free
Bodily analogy;
Blessedly construe
In each syllabic gesture something's praise.
We have mysteriously to be
All beings that we see,
Moving to nights and days:
Grow with a tree,
And speak the universe in paraphrase.

PRAYER

Palm joined to palm,
So not mind only but the hands are trained
To upward attitude, caught and sustained
By wrist and arm:

Reach towards prayer:
The breathing current of the flesh becomes
A soul held gently by the half-crossed thumbs,
Poised in mid-air:

The fingers rise,
Conjoint and mutual, concentrate in grace,
Their slight curves answering the leaning face,
The lidded eyes:

One understands
A vassal pays such homage to his lord,
Kneeling just so while of their own accord
Hands wait for hands:

From a far throne,
Horizon-clouds of ceremonial vesture,
Majesty's hands complete the liegeman's gesture,
And claim their own:

Laid each to each,
Lord's hands hold subject's hands in their broad grasp,
The compact sealed in that enfolding clasp
Of manual speech:

High interleaving
And humble, patterned to the being's core
As Absolution to Confiteor,
Sight to believing,
Rock strata, rose leaves, hinges on the door,
A seamless weaving.

CAROL FOR THE FOUR ELEMENTS

Will you welcome Him, air?
Air ran here and there,
Crying down the long lanes' corridors or rushing
To brush against a cold cheek,
Tangling in the brambles and the held hair,
Answering, "Oh but I am everywhere,
I am His for breathing, as a babe
Gasping first, poor fragment, in a weak wail,
Mourning as the newborn do.
Minister I shall, but surely not in this my dispensation
Is His bailiwick and bourne.
Swift to serve Him truly," with a whistle through
Brown-bare thicketing and thorn,
"Alleluia" whooped the air hallooing like God's
        Gabriel upon a heavenly morning,
Then off off off into the blue.

Will you welcome Him, water?
And water turned at that word,
Curled her long lashes in a laughter lapping,
With her little waves splashing
Like a gentle webfoot bird.
"Glance and mirror I God's glories to the sky,
Where the seas move rocking like a moon-cold cradle
And the ships slide by.
Little fishes spindle-dancing in the weed,
Minnows winking dark and light between the lily roots,
Winnow brindled shallows under His bright Eye.
His for drinking and all human nicety and need,
But not mine, and I must leave Him
Where the final thirsts receive Him
And the long wounds bleed."

Will you welcome Him, fire?
Draw back from the brave heat, heaven-beating spire
And shower of sparks cry out, "Coming we are!
Candle caught in lantern case,
Comfortable glow for glory on a Mother's face,
Or infinite magnificence,
Scimitar of innocence,
White-hot shaft of silver, o the Wise Men's star!
But at best short symbol of His Grace,"
Dying out they whisper,
"Crisp and clinkered cinders in simplicity expire
At His Pleasure. Here is not His Place."

Will you welcome Him, earth,

My own dear element?
And then I heard the heart
Making reply:
I am that earth,
December-cold and dry;
Nothing is left but I
To house His Birth.
On the starved floor,
Dust for the flesh He takes,
Where small chill blunted snakes
Rustle the straw
And spider dangles from the latch.
Earth for His bones,
Some starling rattling like a bag of stones
On the parched thatch.
Nothing delectable,
All dry and cold.
Mine Own Dear Heart, supply
This element,
And, from sterility
Of human mould,
Form, matter, and Thyself
For sacrament.

AT EPIPHANY: FOR A BLIND CHILD

The Child was hooded;
By night; by the protection of His Mother's sleeve;
By a prophetic future, a sign spoken against.

Only by night they came.
No daytime travel: then no star at all.

Their climbing feet stirred the small white cyclamen
On the mountain passes,
And the shooting stars burned green.

In front lay Ramah, the plain of weeping,
The silent swords.

With all about them anguish in the air
(But they rejoicing)

Across whole countries we shall never see,
Tundras of silver sand black fern-fronded under a cold moon,
With angels in their dreams,

With mysterious treasure loaded,
Power and wisdom and pain,

Child, listen and grasp the starry cymbals and bells
With your small ear-drums and your perfect hands—
Your Kings are coming.

EPIPHANY: FOR THE ARTIST

The furred magnificence, the precious stones:
Paint me old men, flesh rags on windy bones

Paint me old men, salt spectres gaunt with years,
Old men and wise; what wisdom but in tears

Old men and wise and wealthy: to accrue
Poverty hinds and herdsmen never knew,
Gifts must be borne in desolation's lieu

Gifts must be borne, offered on broken knees
To Child, Light, God; conceive it how you please
But paint me these.

VIRTUE

Virtue—a small grey stone
Or dead phylactery—
Who'd guess this word unused
Would prove refractory,
And in a sudden flash
Vibrate divinity,
Illuminate the ash
Of school Latinity?
Courage, didn't it mean,
Virtus? Then shaft and facet
Shoot out brilliance between
Explicit and tacit,
Raising to incandescence
The heart's transparency:
Virtue—but that is power,
The being's inner essence,
Its proper potency,
Nine spheres centripetal
In condominium,
Bouquet of star-blue flowers,
Flax and delphinium,
Midnight of morning-glory
Down Heaven's balcony,
A peal of trumpet petals,
Blood-royal indigoes
Whose cordial alchemy,
Attar of spiritual mettle,
Distils to burnet rose
In whose chaste silver cup
Elements cool and fuse
And Virtue's light leaps up—
That word I never use.

Fool, fool and triple fool
That till tonight
Had spent so long at school
Without insight;
In holy dark I heard
Virtue is living art;
Twelvefold the meaninged word,
The sapphire in the heart.
I only see the breach,
The heart unmended,
Small virtue in my speech
So little splendid;
Yet heart and word have cause

Surely for praise
When from their very flaws
Brief poems blaze.

IMMEDIATE ANCESTORS

Before their lives were half-way done
They had lain down between the sheets
Of icy marble, one and one,
To sleep unwanted life away.

From chin to feet slabbed epitaphs sizzled
With virtues, self-drafted (who but they?),
Letters electrically chiselled,
Gold-filled to oust the sun.

Qualities incisively stated, impeccable,
Would render them, they trusted,
Adequately petrified and insulated
Against the lusty grass or springtime spectacle
Of sweet birds mated,
Or those indiscretions, their children.

We, who were eaten alive by their equation,
Deciphering that stone calligraphy,
Quadratics resolving in our own damnation
Unto the third and fourth generation,
Too callow for epigraphy,

Are we to cover up this algebra
With funerary wreaths of our own hair,
Cold ivy's unsuggestive fruit,
Hoared with a frost of bitterness
At our own mutilation,
Lost siblings and shoots?

Yet lastly one shall come
Whose life is half-way done,
Though not with rites you would think suitable,
And at your tomb, long-frozen bed and board,
One of these nights
When the little moon is a soft bright starlight well,
Upon your memory's table
Shall break
A small round honeycake
Baked with sesame seed in a moon of a shell,

And pour out water and oil,
Pious libation
For you alive at last in the fertile soil
And the Three in creation.

ZODIAC SONG

Under which figure was I born,
Scorpio, Cancer, Capricorn?
Well I know, but nothing I'll tell,
For I swing the sky like a lunatic bell
And the waterpot showers its fall of stars
      And the arrow flies.
Under what figure shall I end?
Little I know, but death's a friend
Slipped in with the fish when the deep draughts rise
And the Gemini steep in anemone pools
      Their sleepy eyes.

Under which figure lies my love?
Fearful the scales that dandle above
      Some virginal head;
Yet Aries burns, Leo and Taurus,
Their cries a fierce and fiery chorus,
And five flowered continents lie before us
      Before we're dead.

FOR A FRIEND IN HOSPITAL

Someone gone down:
The first shock worst, the fall
From us and shipboard, gasping in the cold
Immediate convulsive fear to drown;
Not into loneliness but into all,
Souls' ocean concentrated salt, once in
Who knows where his bounds end, the next begin,
Head-over-ears inwhelmed?

Send him some Jonah-fish, so monstrous a surprise
That he might laugh before he disappears;
Lend him that tensile hold
While all the waters close about his ears
And we above
Catch only broken phrases,
Scraps, words misspelled, clothes, letter-shreds washed back
With scales and horns and phosphorescent eyes
Dismembered in the trough of love
Before our taut and wind-burned faces.

In his cold track,
Eyes turned to jewels in that cosmic night
To light the thunderous caverns of the skull,
The flesh packed home with weeds and bladderwrack,
Give him what prayer he needs,
And fifty fathoms deep
What he so long has lacked,
A grace of sleep
As broad as currents sweeping the Azores,
And the whale shadow turquoise on the sandy floors.

And at the end
Where landfall offers in whatever place,
(I shall not compass it, nor any friend
Grind out the flesh for grains and crystal cells
To give him shore and dunes wind-blown through whistling grass
And humming shells and wave-eroded glass
Necklacing blue of the bay with heart-shaped tears)
Give him then welcome,
Little people to finger him, gambol and gape
At so miraculous an escape from living prison,
Or shining ones of whom no language tells.
There let him find, amazed and risen,
Clear water, garments, food, bosom, embrace.

FORGIVENESS

What shall we say it is to be forgiven?—
　　To be in Heaven?
　　Is it to be released?
　　A darkness lighted?
Something of this at least,
　　But more, the marriage-feast.
To be forgiven is to be invited.

What shall we say it is to be forgiven?—
　　To be in Heaven?
To see three rainbows in an hour,
　　That every shower
　　Shone as it rained?
Here was some insight gained.
To be forgiven is to be explained.

What shall we say it is to be forgiven?—
　　To be in Heaven?
To gaze at moon-washed trees
　　Before we slept?
　　A hint from these.
It is a 'yes' that wept,
But not to be accepted: to accept.

What shall we say it is to be forgiven?—
　　To be in Heaven?
　　Is it to meet
A well-beloved on an alien street,
　　Sudden and unexpected?
　　Perhaps connected.
To be forgiven: to be re-directed.

What shall we say it is to be forgiven?—
　　To be in Heaven?
To see, distant but clear,
　　The Promised Land?
Is it Jerusalem and Samarcand?
　　More near.
To be forgiven is to understand.

MUSIC AT A FRIEND'S HOUSE

Astronomer at the bar
Leaned on the balcony,
Watching two fields of power
Where galaxies interfuse,

Measured in ivory tower
Immense celestial views,
Checked automatically
Heart's dull-red dwarfish star.

The universe was clear,
Though swum with cosmic rays;
Astronomer-Royal marked
Their impact on the brain:

Intensity is dark,
Influence falls like rain;
The heart has its own ways
And need not trouble here.

Bivalent time and place:
House-room can heavens provide:
She also has her own
With room for star and guest;

And all the stars had flown
Indoors and come to rest,
And leaves that fell outside
Came down from outer space.

Where system system nears,
Position need not change
Where each is circumspect
Of other's frame of star:

Or say love and respect
Supply the near and far,
And no heart's hum derange
The consort of the spheres.

But if another kind
Of music intervene
(So lately I have learned)
No universe can hold;

Heart-cycles are unturned,
Contingencies unfold
Utterly unforeseen
By cogitating mind.

This will bring down
Even astronomers
Who thought all music theirs
And meant to keep it so;

Deny heart any shares,
Sprawled star-wise in a glow
On ivory balusters
In an old dressing-gown.

Tentative the first phrases
She plays downstairs apart;
They sing about the room
Like the small seraphim;

Then in the gloom
Where inner star burned dim,
The heart the heart the heart
Explodes and blazes.

A flash, mind turned to say
With sudden anxious stare,
Irrational swift light
And nothing will remain;

The body from its night
Sent meteors of pain,
The heart's black wildfire glare
Taking the breath away.

The breastbone took the thrust
  Of solar light and heat,
    White-hot the heart expanding
    To global fiery ball;

    Driven on to the landing,
    Head leaned against the wall,
  Darkened with urge to weep
And clouds of stinging dust.

Half-blind astronomy
  Still tries to sound:
    Can this be culpable?
    Desire? deception?

    Consult the oracle,
    Starry conception:
  And then heart found
A new autonomy.

Mind, body, wholly still,
  Wait for an answer,
    Heard the heart chime
    An orbit through the pain;

    Resolve in time
    The duly questioning brain,
  Move like a dancer
Whom images fulfil.

Atom—so sang the heart—
  Spins in a glassy wire
    Ghost of an involute rose
    As dark and fierce as this;

    Snap it, there blows
    A budding storm of bliss,
  Black petals pricked with fire,
Creation's counterpart.

Thorned whorl of power,
High cloud-inverted bell,
Wringing up land and sea
For substance, dewy salt,

Bears without fault
That consummate energy
Which kernels every cell,
Heart, star and flower . . .

Somewhere a rose, a star,
Astronomer, a fool,
Accepts an unknown grace
Of joy too great to bear;

With closed averted face
Expects the cadenced air;
Heart too will cool
And leave behind no scar.

The airy notes disperse,
Owing no explanation;
Folded the rose, the word;
Stars drop like autumn leaves.

All vision is absurd,
Yet may this be received,
Wayward illumination,
In your broad universe.

GARLAND FOR A SCIENTIST

A little chilly for the Nine today?
Dew-powdered to a crisp rococo grey
    The godhead's laurelled curls;
    And are you cold, poor girls,
Bare-footed in this hyperborean May?

Faint, rosy, patient—what is it they see?
That threadbare figure by the flowering tree?
    "Naming is not enough,"—
    Dusts pollen off his cuff—
"We need a different taxonomy."

His rivals thought he'd found an ABC,
To tidy up, say, the *Rosaceae*,
    The learned mind too stiff
    To ply his hieroglyph,
Sex as an intellectual master-key.

Shadowy still he waits the box and bay,
The fitting honours for the lord Linné,
    Whose systematics yield
    The nature of that field
Where the Nine Muses with Apollo play.

I

POET TO SCIENTIST

Yours the intensity of perfect mind,
    The virgin light no prism can dispart,
The lattice where true tenses are declined.

Your instruments are crystals and cold beams,
    And the integrities of head and heart
Solemnize marriage at their last extremes.

Loving's our work, it seems; but where's the nerve
    To conjugate your white near-infinite speed
With my wet rainbow's broken-coloured curve?

Yet by your light I find: Idea's bed,
    Where at full stretch of soul our thoughts may breed,
Is ultra-violet and infra-red.

ORPHEUS I

To sightlessness is love consigned,
And, if it love, the thinking mind
Consents no less to being blind:

So the musician at the strings,
Withdrawn from all surrounding things,
Attends to what the music sings:

Orpheus descends, as he was taught,
Towards his dear remembered thought,
But lost in seeing what he sought.

Intensity surpassing sight,
Shadows of sensing hands invite
The concentration of delight

In all whose thought and love, compact,
Feel with a long and fingering tact
For outline of an artefact:

Orpheus in minds undoes the curse
That splits us into prose or verse;
And, shaping, finds the universe.

III

ORPHEUS II

There is a long music.
It comes from a severed head
Clutched in the tree roots.

The voyage down-river
Was traced by the mouth that bled
Its undrowned singing.

Mysterious if that skull,
All its dark sayings are said
For innocent people.

Should you ask understanding,
Go living, my soul, to the dead,
And see what happens.

IV

DATA

Poem is something that is made,
    The ruined house under the rain,
Whose sky-bound staircase balustrade
    Ends in the infinite inane;

With everything five wits contain,
    Poem is something that is made,
Gaslight through foul or shattered pane,
    When heart begins to be afraid;

No smallest fact but must be laid
    Along the grain the nerves provide;
Poem is something that is made,
    Together with the world outside;

Tables and chairs and cold and pain,
    So still and shapely, have obeyed;
Sense is the senses' one refrain:
They neither falter nor explain:
That is the burden of the brain.
    Poem is something that is made.

V
WORDS AND STARS

If God had spoken stars in the beginning,
Man's mind no less obeyed its tendencies,
Astronomers soon busy underpinning
Grammar and syntax of those sentences;

Astrology could offer only fancy,
The incantation and the sophist's trick;
Poets divined, in place of necromancy,
Superlative sidereal rhetoric.

To logic, metaphor is mere annoyance;
Lone image is anarchical and shoddy;
Their dialectic offers no advance.

What speculation in that high flamboyance?
What wedding heavenly mind to heavenly body,
The figure in the discourse and the dance?

VI

WAYS AND MEANS

Only angelic thoughts may climb that ladder,
Dancing to God, through skies of milk and madder,
    Logic's ascension.
Others must greenly grow, sprung tendrils hoping
Trellis of air, Jack's beanstalk slowly groping
    Its own extension.
Far off I see Heaven's ultimate arbours shine,
Where line and leaf geometries combine,
    Metamorphosis
Of metaphor's and dialectic's loss:
Chaste frame of silver squares, and all across,
    Passion of roses.

VII

THINKING

Whatever thinks the crystal, has been taught
    Perfected plan,
  Can flawlessly rehearse
  Much of the universe.
This is a harder thought:
    To be a man.

Plant-thought designed
    The intricated mesh,
  Giving itself the power
  To realize leaf and flower.
Man only feels his mind
    In-fibrilled in the flesh.

Beast-thoughts have grace,
    Whose body is their brain.
  Manthought lies buried deep
  Where dumb the organs sleep;
Gleams struggle to his face;
    Then blind again.

Mind—fluted gem,
    Flushed trumpet-vines where dart
  Exquisite long-tongued words,
  Hawkmoths and hummingbirds—
O choose, rather than them,
    Man's heavy heart.

VIII
THE TWO KINDS

I have sat down with the Entities at table,
Eaten with them the meal of ceremony,
And they were stamped with jewels, and intuned
    God's ordered praises.

But now the Activities hand me to the dancing,
Brown naked bodies lithe and crimson-necklaced,
And tambourines besiege the darkened altars,
    In what God's honour?

BUD AND TRIVIUM

Never again lay ear against a shell:
  Already something stirs, or so it seems.
Listen only to stones who cannot tell,
  They sleep so fast, their stiff inaudible dreams,
Whispered through walls of bone into your skull.

For yesterday a bud began to speak.
  (So young? but offshoot of a classic line
Half-infinite to our poor Latin and Greek,
  Each plant a slip of immemorial vine,
And even more than we, both young and old.)

Conservative in what it had to teach,
  The mode Socratic and the theme Scholastic,
Actions and figures as implicit speech,
  From which organic *Trivium* green and plastic
As its own substance it deduced ourselves.

Showed three relations: first, that of survival,
  The *Dialectic* in the thorn and claw,
Bodily argument with every rival
  As the inflexible ruling of the law.
Here Darwin stopped, but there are two to come:

For *Rhetoric* plays with natural selection,
  Hyperbole swims and flies in red and gold;
Ingenious living similes for protection;
  Beauty's unnecessary manifold;
And *Grammar* is the dance of living form.

Was this once known and framed to education,
  High ancient code, we fools have lost the clues?
Master-vision or mere hallucination,
  Organon bedded crackling like a fuse
In the damp innocence of a crinkled bud?

Suppose it opens as we wait before it,
  A huge gold circle with a face and eyes,
Would it begin to speak? best to implore it,
  'Moon, make no mouth whose monstrous prophecies
Blow like God's horns as we go down to dust'?

Or would it simply show, in slow dilating,
    Plato and Aristotle closely curled
Inside a yellow roseleaf, speculating
    That language is the nature of the world,
And all philosophy a flowering thought?

Fierce, honey-throated, formalized, prolific,
    Anticipate in our most human powers,
The poet but a speaking hieroglyphic
    In one whole universe of continual flowers,
Shall we run, weeping, throw away our life?

Or gather little children in a ring,
And blossom into oracles and sing
That mind and word is every living thing?

X

IDEAS

The coming of new forms
Is priestly and war-like; doubled they campaign,
Ringing, besiege the mind with holy storms

Till shouts and trumpets crack
The glassy air; fortifications spill,
And we lie open, to fury and to sack

And then to all the expanses of the plain,
The world's wide landscape suddenly appears,
And nine huge stars waiting above the hill
Will march through walls of clay-dust to the brain
And camp there, silent, leaning on their spears.

ORPHEUS III

He sees over his shoulder
  Flowers, not her;
Scarcely a second older,
  For still they stir;
Not asphodel but colder,
  And sharp as myrrh.

Half-roused from holy sleeping
  Their pallor flames
To urge upon his keeping
  A lover's claims.
Sunlit, he stumbles, weeping,
  To give them names.

ORPHEUS IV

Let him chord up the stars,
Sweeten the salt sea,
Answer with his heartstrings
For our sterility—
  So the wild women cried,
  And Orpheus died.
Stars were strung to sound,
Waves turned red,
And the wild women, appeased,
Went home to supper and bed.
Far out, what echoes brood
One ravished head?

XIII

GENESIS

Poet by poet launched upon that sea.
This was before the moon was, or the land.
Everything in a moving patience waited
To be created—

Solitary were they borne
On those immense waters
Breathing and profound,
(How many drowned),
The mind, the Mind,
Under this presence contemplated—

In darkness but for stars
That crowded, jostled, stabbed and showered and rang,
The tideless ocean tingled and pulsated,
A million working surfaces for light,
And by those influences impregnated—

Of World and Mind
Poet by poet said
No thing is only dead
And nothing unrelated.

A SEQUENCE

I

Under the frost fell
Of winter drere,
Heart houseth safe and well,
Withouten fear.
What though it pinchèd be,
Long, long opposèd
By storms and enmitie?
Like frozen bud i' th' tree
Abideth in suretie
The heart beclosèd.

Only when in May-bliss,
Under the sweet sun,
Each creature gladsome is
That winter be outrun,
When the soft air of spring
His balm shaketh,
For love the small birds sing,
The new leaves are breaking,
Even so, with everie thing,
The heart breaketh.

II

The clarity of love
Lust makes opaque;
The flesh is set between
For mercy's sake.

Hold fast the sense
With all its burning ache,
For where desire is not,
The heart will break.

The charity of love
No vessel can comprise:
O clutch the breast for pain,
And tears run from the eyes.

III

One perfect note
    From violin:
The glass in fragments
    Fallen in.

There was no fault,
    There was no flaw;
Each nature to
    Its proper law.

No mystery even
    To brood upon—
The crystal shivered
    And the sound gone.

MOURNING DOVES

To give the spirit ease,
These are the quiet angels
Among the flowering trees.
    To heart that would rejoice
    In loveliness it sees,
    Lending their gentle voice
    Of lamentation.
Glimpsed now and then aground,
Lavender and blue-grey—
Not these. Only the sound.
    The happy doves,
    Some other mourns, not they,
    They have their loves.
    We say: imagination;
Yet silently attest,
Innocently expressed,
That constant desolation.

MIGRATING JUNCOS

March snow
Over the whole ground.
What though?
Newly a-visit,
Exquisite voices sound,
Quick airy company,
Whose gray-blue backs and wings
Take colour of sky,
White belly snow-reflected;
Twig-perched, kneehigh,
Through icicle fringe sun-burning,
One sings and sings.

Soft, musical, that cry
Shivers for joy, not cold.
He pipes, his fellows dance
(Darting, returning)
The sun, the snow,
Earth ritual perfected
Into birds,
Whilst I, humanly, slow,
Offer up words.

PHOENIX AND UNICORN

I

True hearts denied
   Their sacrificial fires
Give one another
   Only fabulous beasts
No ruddy lions throng
   Their hymeneal feasts
Tigers nor white-maned horses
   The splendid sires

Will you accept
   A unicorn perhaps
Whose milky-clouded radiance
   Rare as your own
Exhales faint lonely sweetness
   Of flesh and bone
Nourished upon the mountains'
   Chaste stony laps

All is most dear and true, all is most good.
Your phoenix waits you deeper in the wood.

II. EASTER UNICORN

Church schools teach nothing about unicorns.
Some fierce old Gospel blazoned red and green,
By this do we interpret, by this learn?

We hunt him on the instant he is seen.
For hunger. Lust to have. Hate to destroy.
Scenting him out: this is our love, our joy.
In the deep woods halloo of silver horns.

Light hoofs for love grow heavy on the leaves.

Shouts dinning, mêlée of arms, flushed faces burn,
And oh the bright blood down that moony flank.

The passage next is dark: death and a quest.

Follows only the blank heart's cry: Oh when
The springtime flowers across the lovely land,
Sun, moon, in gold and silver sarabande,
Unicorn grieves, loves, resting in his pen?

III. A TALE THAT IS TOLD

At that high point they vanished, two abreast,
Climbing the sunward rocks to the Phoenix' Nest.

Scarcely expecting that one sunset bird;
There had been lesser tales that they had heard,

How from rock-crevices wild honey drips,
Out of burst combs, on upturned throats and lips.

Their footsteps raised small dust-clouds in the place,
Bee-debris, powder of wing and carapace.

It seems they halted, gazing, side by side:
Rocks split in pain; black sugar long since dried.

Nothing but rumours now; but it appears
They settled to wait out the thousand years.

Honeyless, dreaming, bone to bone they lie.
They waken only at the Phoenix' cry
Who find to love as lonely as to die.

Dream not the olive's fat
Drops benison to the dust
Or vines bestow their must
On any but the vat.
Here the unfriended ground
Gold-purple thistle pranks,
And arid lizards pound
Lozenge-striated flanks.

Here umber ploughlands trudge
Devoid of tenderness,
And in blue heaven's largesse
The beasts, the women drudge.
Here birds are daily shot
Out of the scented pines.
On the hard skyrim squat
The gloom-blue Appenines.

Meet, then, to meet it here:
The overflowing, whole,
The heartfelt, anxious, sole,
Deep, tender, none more near,
The sealed with self, the sheer
Longdrawn—and long abhorred—
Immeasurably dear
Lovelonging of my Lord.

Not in a greener tract
Where nature can respond;
Least in a lover's bond
Whose sweetness must distract.
See now more wholly apt,
Francesco limps in rags,
Hangs Benedetto, rapt,
On Subiaco crags.